A Guide to Executing Change for Managers

Participant Workbook

Wayne R. Davis

T0344957

Pfeiffer

A Wiley Imprint

www.pfeiffer.com

Published by Pfeiffer
An Imprint of Wiley
989 Market Street, San Francisco, CA 94103-1741
www.pfeiffer.com

For additional copies/bulk purchases of this book in the U.S. please contact 800-274-4434.

Pfeiffer books and products are available through most bookstores. To contact Pfeiffer directly call our Customer Care Department within the U.S. at 800-274-4434, outside the U.S. at 317-572-3985, fax 317-572-4002, or visit www.pfeiffer.com.

Pfeiffer also publishes its books in a variety of electronic formats. Some content that appears in print may not be available in electronic books.

Managers: Participant Workbook ISBN: 978-0-470-40003-6

Acquiring Editor: Holly Allen
Marketing Manager: Tolu Babalola
Director of Development: Kathleen Dolan Davies
Developmental Editor: Susan Rachmeler
Production Editor: Michael Kay
Editor: Rebecca Taff
Assistant Editor: Marisa Kelley
Manufacturing Supervisor: Becky Morgan

Printed in the United States of America

Printing   10 9 8 7 6 5 4 3 2 1

Contents

Overview

Your manager has distributed this workbook to you and other members of your department, work group, or team. You will use this workbook as a resource and guide in upcoming meetings with your manager, in change workshops, and for personal development, reflection, and action planning.

Two of the activities—1, Change Style Assessment, and 3, My Future—will be completed as pre-work. You will meet with your manager prior to completing Activity 3, as he or she will provide necessary input for this activity. Activity 1 you will complete on your own. Both should be done prior to attending the Managers Workshop.

Change Style Assessment

Instructions

The Change Style Assessment consists of twenty-one questions. You complete the assessment using sentence completion and checking the phrase that best describes you.

Please answer every question. Do not leave any question unanswered.

If you have difficulty selecting a single answer, ask yourself which response would be most natural or likely for you at work.

There are no *wrong answers* to these questions, so base your response on how you are today, not how you think you should be or would like to be in the future.

Example

1. When planning change, I want to know . . .

　　a. *What do we need to do to be competitive?*

✗ b. *What people needs are being considered?*

　　c. *What has worked in the past?*

　　d. *What opportunities will the change create?*

Change Style Assessment

1. When planning change, I want to know . . .

___a. What do we need to do to be competitive?

___b. What people needs are being considered?

___c. What has worked in the past?

___d. What opportunities will the change create?

2. If an important decision is to be made, I . . .

___a. Think it through completely before deciding.

___b. Go with my gut instincts.

___c. Consider the impact it will have on other people before deciding.

___d. Run it by someone whose opinion I respect before deciding.

3. During change, I want to know . . .

___a. How will the change affect people?

___b. Who is committed to the change?

___c. Why are we making the change?

___d. What needs to be done?

4. If I am having a conflict with a co-worker or customer, I . . .

___a. Try to help the situation along by focusing on the positive.

___b. Stay calm and try to understand the cause of the conflict.

___c. Try to avoid discussing the issue causing the conflict.

___d. Confront it right away so that it can bet resolved as soon as possible.

5. My preferred role during change is to . . .

___a. Take charge.

___b. Build consensus.

___c. Work behind the scenes.

___d. Pay attention to the details.

6. My motto is . . .

___a. "Don't speak ill of boss or colleagues."

___b. "Let's do it right, no matter what it takes."

___c. "Don't bug me with rules, limits, and details."

___d. "Let's get it done and get it done now."

7. I approach change . . .

____a. With caution: "Is this just another change for change's sake?"

____b. As necessary to achieve goals.

____c. With enthusiasm for new opportunities.

____d. With concern about how the change will affect responsibilities, relationships and culture

8. The word that most accurately describes me during change is . . .

____a. Persuasive.

____b. Cautious.

____c. Loyal.

____d. Commanding.

9. When a co-worker or customer is explaining a problem to me, I . . .

____a. Try to understand and empathize with how he or she is feeling.

____b. Look for the specific facts pertaining to the situation.

____c. Listen carefully for the main issue so that I can find a solution.

____d. Use my body language and tone of voice to show her or him that I understand.

10. When attending training programs or presentations, I . . .

____a. Become bored if the person moves too slowly.

____b. Try to be supportive of the speaker, knowing how hard the job is.

____c. Want it to be entertaining as well as informative.

____d. Look for the logic behind what the speaker is saying.

11. When I want to put my point across to others, I . . .

____a. Listen to the individual's point of view first and then express my ideas gently.

____b. Strongly state my opinion so that person knows where I stand.

____c. Try to persuade him or her without being too forceful.

____d. Explain the thinking and logic behind what I am saying.

12. It is important for me to know . . .

____a. What is the realistic reason for the change?

____b. What is expected of me personally?

____c. What has to be accomplished?

____d. Will I be involved with new people, ideas and initiatives?

13. I set goals and objectives at work that I . . .

    ____a. Think I can realistically attain.

    ____b. Feel are challenging and would be exciting to achieve.

    ____c. Need to achieve as part of a bigger objective.

    ____d. Think will make me feel good when I achieve them.

14. When explaining a problem to a co-worker from whom I need help, I . . .

    ____a. Explain the problem in as much detail as possible.

    ____b. Sometimes exaggerate to make my point.

    ____c. Try to explain how the problem makes me feel.

    ____d. Explain how I would like the problem to be solved.

15. Words that best describe me are . . .

    ____a. Outgoing, enthusiastic, and creative.

    ____b. Diplomatic, dependable, and sensitive.

    ____c. Serious, quiet, and business-like.

    ____d. Decisive, forceful, and blunt.

16. When I am behind on a project and feel pressure to get it done, I . . .

    ____a. Make a list of everything I need to do, in what order, by when.

    ____b. Block out everything else and focus 100 percent on the work I need to do.

    ____c. Become anxious and have a hard time focusing on my work.

    ____d. Set a deadline to complete the project and do it.

17. When I feel verbally attacked by a customer or a co-worker, I . . .

    ____a. Tell the person to stop.

    ____b. Feel hurt but usually don't say anything about it to him or her.

    ____c. Ignore her or his anger and try to focus on the facts of the situation.

    ____d. Let the person know in strong terms that I don't like his or her behavior.

18. I am most interested in . . .

____a. A warm social environment with secure working conditions where my loyalty and teaming skills are valued.

____b. A predictable environment with set rules and procedures where I can use my logic and diagnostic skills.

____c. An environment that is constantly changing, where I can affect growth, efficiency, and production.

____d. A friendly, collaborative environment where I can use my creative and social skills to benefit the company.

19. My communication style is . . .

____a. Fast-paced, enthusiastic, big-picture oriented.

____b. Business-focused, to-the-point, authoritative.

____c. Personal, soft spoken, good listener.

____d. Formal, structured, facts, and detail focused.

20. What is important to me is . . .

____a. Job security, cooperation, and approval.

____b. No surprises, ample resources, and alone time.

____c. Challenging goals, control, and power.

____d. Variety, new possibilities, and flexibility.

21. What I can do to be more effective is . . .

____a. Take more risks, decide faster, and monitor my perfectionism.

____b. Look before I leap, improve my time management, and be more objective.

____c. Disagree when necessary, develop greater assertiveness, and be more open to change.

____d. Ask, listen more, and monitor my high expectation of self and others.

Scoring

Referring to your responses to the questions on the Change Style Assessment, circle the appropriate letter that corresponds to your answer to each question.

Question Number	Collaborator	Protector	Initiator	Questioner
1	d	b	a	c
2	d	c	b	a
3	b	a	d	c
4	a	b	d	c
5	b	c	a	d
6	c	a	d	b
7	c	d	b	a
8	a	c	d	b
9	d	a	c	b
10	c	b	a	d
11	c	a	b	d
12	d	b	c	a
13	b	d	c	a
14	b	c	d	a
15	a	b	d	c
16	d	c	b	a
17	d	b	a	c
18	d	a	c	b
19	a	c	b	d
20	d	a	c	b
21	b	c	d	a
Total				

Now count the number of letters you circled in each column and record the answer in the appropriate box. To verify your work, the sum of the four boxes should be equal to 21.

Your highest score indicates the style you most closely identify with.

During the next activity, as a group, you'll find the total number of participants who identify with each style. You'll also calculate the percentage each style comprises of the group overall.

Notes

_____

_____

_____

_____

_____

_____

_____

_____

_____

_____

_____

_____

_____

_____

_____

_____

_____

_____

_____

_____

2

My Profile—Change and Me

WHEN EVERYONE IN your department has completed the Change Style Assessment, each person will report out his or her type. Sum and calculate the percentage for each category and enter the results in the appropriate boxes below for your group.

Collaborator	Protector	Initiator	Questioner
Count:	Count:	Count:	Count:
Percentage:	Percentage:	Percentage:	Percentage:

Change Style Map

Change Role: Preferred role during change
Orientation: Focus during change
Openness to Change: Attitude about change
Emotional Expression: Degree of emotion expressed during change

11

	Collaborator		Protector
Count:		**Count:**	
Percentage:		**Percentage:**	

Characteristics	**Characteristics**
Assertive, confident and outgoing	Diplomatic and dependable
Visionaries who focus on new possibilities	Good listeners
Excited and optimistic about change	Can be indecisive in situations that involve change and risk

Contributions During Change

Collaborator:
Use creative talents and social skills to build good personal relationships that will benefit the company

Excels at introducing and gaining buy-in for change

Comfortable with ambiguity; can see both sides of an issue

Protector:
Loyal to organization and colleagues. When committed to an initiative willingly does back-stage work necessary to complete the task.

Provides insight on the potential affected of change on employees, clients, constituents, and other stakeholders.

Sensitive to the people side of doing business.

Needs During Change

Collaborator:
Help with organization, structure, schedules and deadlines

Support the ability to sell others on the change initiative by providing them the facts and details they need to validate their message

Protector:
Personal reassurance and sincere expression of appreciation

Clear instructions

Help with priorities and meeting deadlines

To be probed for their input and opinions

Change Tips for Collaborators

When presenting the change message, don't exaggerate.

Validate the change message with facts and logic.

Admit when you don't know the answer; don't "wing it."

Change Tips for Protectors

Be more assertive. Speak up. Express your opinions.

Develop emotional boundaries.

Consider the benefits of change.

Try being more open to new ways of doing things.

Count:		Count:	
Percentage:	**Initiator**	**Percentage:**	**Questioner**

Characteristics

Change drivers

Goal and action-oriented

Enjoy variety and an environment that is continuously changing

Push for speedy results and the bottom line

Contributions During Change

Business-focused and decisive, gets things done

Practical problem-solver

Works well in crisis, fast-paced, and turn-around situations

Needs During Change

Support in implementing change

Others to provide accurate data and details

Help with the people side of change

Answers to what are the costs? What will the solution do? How soon can it be done?

Change Tips for Initiators

Practice being more patient with those who hesitate to accept change.

Modify your expectations periodically.

Your high expectations may not be realistic for others who need more information and time. Others may find your approach pushy, become disillusioned, and lose motivation.

Characteristics

Serious and industrious

Analytical and methodical

Objective and business-focused

Have difficulty accepting change unless they understand the purpose and rationale for it

Contributions During Change

Listens well and catches inconsistencies

Provide planning, organization, and structure

Keeps a keen eye on quality control and standards

Needs During Change

Ample time to make decisions

Limited surprises

Frequent communication with specifics

Help with indecisiveness and time management

Change Tips for Questioners

Practice being more flexible when applying rules and structure.

Try being more comfortable with and more optimistic about change.

Monitor your need for perfection.

During change, expect and accept time limits on data collecting and planning.

The facilitator will then chart the group's results on a Change Assessment Graph, a sample of which is shown below. Record the group's actual results on the blank graph that follows.

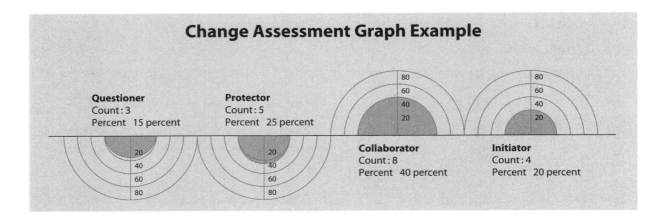

Change Assessment Graph for Your Department

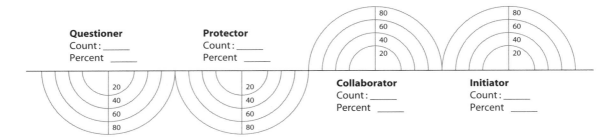

Respond to the following six questions individually and be prepared to discuss your responses with the whole group.

1. What do you conclude from the change assessment results?

2. What are the people challenges for you and your department?

3. What training interventions are needed to address the issues identified by the change assessment?

4. How will you use the "contributions during change" characteristics to execute effective change?

5. How will you address the unique "needs" attributes of each change type?

6. How will you use the information to build a more effective department, work group, or team during change?

Notes

_____

_____

_____

_____

_____

_____

_____

_____

_____

_____

_____

_____

_____

_____

_____

_____

_____

_____

_____

_____

3

My Future—What's Ahead? What Will Change?

YOUR MANAGER IS the primary resource for this exercise and will provide guidance in determining the effects and impact of the change initiative on the eight areas of change.

Your manager will provide specific information for you as it relates to the following areas of change:

1. My Job Description

2. My Work Activities

3. My Practices and Processes

4. My Reporting Structure

5. My Career Path

6. My Skills and Competencies

7. My Rewards and Recognition

8. My Opportunities for Success

Based on the information you received from your manager, please complete the series of eight worksheets. For each worksheet, you will do the following:

1. Answer the questions: What will change? What are the new opportunities? What are the new challenges?

2. Indicate your perception (positive, neutral, negative) by checking the appropriate box of how this specific change will affect you personally.

3. Complete an action plan needed to address the specific change.

The activity also includes one blank worksheet you can use to address an additional area of your choice.

When you've completed all the worksheets for yourself, complete the overall perception of change summary by adding the number of plus, zero, and minus symbols from all the worksheets.

1. My Job Description

What will change? _____

_____

_____

What are the new opportunities? _____

_____

_____

What are the new challenges? _____

_____

_____

My overall perception of how this change will affect me personally.

+	0	–

Action Plan

What do I need to do?	When do I need to do it?	What resources do I need?
_____	_____	_____
_____	_____	_____
_____	_____	_____
_____	_____	_____
_____	_____	_____

Notes: _____

_____

_____

_____

2. My Work Activities

What will change? _____

_____

_____

What are the new opportunities? _____

_____

_____

What are the new challenges? _____

_____

_____

My overall perception of how this change will affect me personally.

+	0	−

Action Plan

What do I need to do?	When do I need to do it?	What resources do I need?
_____	_____	_____
_____	_____	_____
_____	_____	_____
_____	_____	_____

Notes: _____

_____

_____

3. My Practices and Processes

What will change? _____

_____

_____

What are the new opportunities? _____

_____

_____

What are the new challenges? _____

_____

_____

My overall perception of how this change will affect me personally.

+	0	−

Action Plan

What do I need to do?	When do I need to do it?	What resources do I need?
_____	_____	_____
_____	_____	_____
_____	_____	_____
_____	_____	_____
_____	_____	_____

Notes:_____

_____

_____

_____

4. My Reporting Structure

What will change? _____

_____

_____

What are the new opportunities? _____

_____

_____

What are the new challenges? _____

_____

_____

My overall perception of how this change will affect me personally.

+	0	−

Action Plan

What do I need to do?	When do I need to do it?	What resources do I need?
_____	_____	_____
_____	_____	_____
_____	_____	_____
_____	_____	_____

Notes: _____

_____

_____

5. My Career Path

What will change? _____

_____

_____

What are the new opportunities? _____

_____

_____

What are the new challenges? _____

_____

_____

My overall perception of how this change will affect me personally.

+	0	−

Action Plan

What do I need to do?	When do I need to do it?	What resources do I need?
_____	_____	_____
_____	_____	_____
_____	_____	_____
_____	_____	_____
_____	_____	_____

Notes:_____

_____

_____

_____

6. My Skills and Competencies

What will change? _____

_____

_____

What are the new opportunities? _____

_____

_____

What are the new challenges? _____

_____

_____

My overall perception of how this change will affect me personally.

+	0	−

Action Plan

What do I need to do?	When do I need to do it?	What resources do I need?
_____	_____	_____
_____	_____	_____
_____	_____	_____
_____	_____	_____
_____	_____	_____

Notes:_____

_____

_____

_____

7. My Rewards and Recognition

What will change? _____

_____

_____

What are the new opportunities? _____

_____

_____

What are the new challenges? _____

_____

_____

My overall perception of how this change will affect me personally.

+	0	–

Action Plan

What do I need to do?	When do I need to do it?	What resources do I need?
_____	_____	_____
_____	_____	_____
_____	_____	_____
_____	_____	_____
_____	_____	_____

Notes:_____

_____

_____

_____

8. My Opportunities for Success

What will change? _____

_____

_____

What are the new opportunities? _____

_____

_____

What are the new challenges? _____

_____

_____

My overall perception of how this change will affect me personally.

+	0	–

Action Plan

What do I need to do?	When do I need to do it?	What resources do I need?
_____	_____	_____
_____	_____	_____
_____	_____	_____
_____	_____	_____
_____	_____	_____

Notes:_____

_____

_____

_____

My ...

What will change? _____

_____

_____

What are the new opportunities? _____

_____

_____

What are the new challenges? _____

_____

_____

My overall perception of how this change will affect me personally.

+	0	–

Action Plan

What do I need to do?	When do I need to do it?	What resources do I need?
_____	_____	_____
_____	_____	_____
_____	_____	_____
_____	_____	_____
_____	_____	_____

Notes: _____

_____

_____

_____

Overall Perception of Change Summary

Next, add the number of plusses, zeros, and minuses from the above activity and enter the totals here.

+	_____
0	_____
–	_____

Notes

4

Indicators of Change

COMPLETE THIS ACTIVITY by reading each statement and checking the column that represents your perception of the change initiative's effect on you personally. Add comments as indicated.

Will I ...	No	Yes	If Yes, Explain
Be in a new team or workgroup?			
Serve a different internal client?			
Serve a different external client?			

Will the ...	No	Slightly	Significantly	Massively	If Other Than No, Explain
Inputs I deal with change?					
Data or services I render change?					
Outputs I create or perform change?					
Way I contribute change?					

Will the manner in which information is ...	No	Slightly	Significantly	Massively	If Other Than No, Explain
Produced, gathered, or stored change?					
Recorded, managed, or used change?					
Reported or presented change?					
Analyzed or differentiated change?					
Interpreted or diagnosed change?					
Shared or propagated change?					
Acted on change?					

Next, add the number of checks and enter the result in the appropriate column.

Indicators of Change Summary

No	Yes	Slightly	Significantly	Massively

Notes

_____

_____

_____

_____

_____

_____

_____

_____

_____

_____

_____

_____

_____

_____

_____

_____

_____

_____

_____

5

My Praxis Chart

GO BACK TO the My Future exercise (Number 3) in this workbook. Review the My Work Activities (Number 2) and the My Practices and Processes (Number 3) worksheets.

1. Complete this exercise by listing each **work activity** and each **practice and process** in one of the lettered sections below.

2. For each activity/practice/process, check the box that most clearly defines what you need to do to affect the change.

3. For each activity/practice/process, describe the response required by you to successfully address the change.

A.

1. Activity/Practice/Process _____

_____

_____

_____

(✓)	More of This	Less of This	Do This Differently	Stop Doing This	Start Doing This
2.					

3. Response _____

_____

_____

B.

1. Activity/Practice/Process _____

_____

_____

_____

(✓)	More of This	Less of This	Do This Differently	Stop Doing This	Start Doing This
2.					

3. Response _____

_____

_____

C.

1. Activity/Practice/Process _____

_____

_____

_____

(✓)	More of This	Less of This	Do This Differently	Stop Doing This	Start Doing This
2.					

3. Response _____

_____

_____

D.

1. Activity/Practice/Process _____

_____

_____

_____

(✓)	More of This	Less of This	Do This Differently	Stop Doing This	Start Doing This
2.					

3. Response _____

_____

_____

E.

1. Activity/Practice/Process _____

_____

_____

_____

(✓)	More of This	Less of This	Do This Differently	Stop Doing This	Start Doing This
2.					

3. Response _____

_____

_____

F.

   1. Activity/Practice/Process _____

_____

_____

_____

(✓)	More of This	Less of This	Do This Differently	Stop Doing This	Start Doing This
2.					

   3. Response _____

_____

_____

G.

   1. Activity/Practice/Process _____

_____

_____

_____

(✓)	More of This	Less of This	Do This Differently	Stop Doing This	Start Doing This
2.					

   3. Response _____

_____

_____

H.

1. Activity/Practice/Process _____

_____

_____

_____

(✓)	More of This	Less of This	Do This Differently	Stop Doing This	Start Doing This
2.					

3. Response _____

_____

_____

I.

1. Activity/Practice/Process _____

_____

_____

_____

(✓)	More of This	Less of This	Do This Differently	Stop Doing This	Start Doing This
2.					

3. Response _____

_____

_____

J.

1. Activity/Practice/Process _____

_____

_____

_____

(✓)	More of This	Less of This	Do This Differently	Stop Doing This	Start Doing This
2.					

3. Response _____

_____

_____

Add the number of checks marks in each category and enter the total in the appropriate space below.

More of This	_____
Less of This	_____
Do This Differently	_____
Stop Doing This	_____
Start Doing This	_____

Notes

_____

_____

_____

_____

_____

_____

_____

_____

_____

_____

_____

_____

_____

_____

_____

_____

_____

_____

_____

_____

6

My Scorecard—How I Perceive That This Change Initiative Will Affect Me

RECORD THE RESULTS from the "My Future—What's Ahead? What Will Change?" activity here.

+	_____
0	_____
–	_____

Record the results from the "Indicators of Change" activity here.

No	Yes	Slightly	Significantly	Massively

Record the results from the "My Praxis Chart" activity here.

More of This	_____
Less of This	_____
Do This Differently	_____
Stop Doing This	_____
Start Doing This	_____

Notes

7

My Change Meter—None, Some, Lots, Massive

DRAW A NEEDLE on the gauge below to best represent your view of the impact this change initiative will have on you personally.

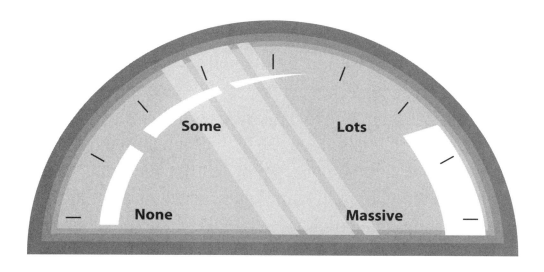

Notes

8

My Feedback—Observations and Needs

Observations

PLACE A CHECK mark in the box below to indicate your perception of the planned change process in each case. Also, add any additional observations you feel are important.

My instinct tells me this change initiative will:

	(✓)	Observation
a.		Fall short of expectations
b.		Be very successful
c.		Have a negative effect on customers
d.		Start with a bang and then sputter and crash
e.		Lead us in a wrong direction
f.		Provide a new and compelling vision
g.		
h.		
i.		

Needs

Place a check mark in the box below to indicate your area of need during the planned change effort. Also add any additional needs you feel have not been addressed, whether you check them or not.

To be successful, I will need:

	(✓)	I Will Need
a.		More clarity of vision
b.		More leadership direction
c.		More executive communication
d.		More training in change
e.		More training in new skills and competencies
f.		More time to get it done
g.		More resources and budget
h.		
i.		

Notes

_____

_____

_____

_____

_____

_____

_____

_____

_____

_____

_____

_____

_____

_____

_____

_____

_____

_____

_____

9

My Summary and Next Steps

My Challenges

_____

_____

My Priorities

_____

_____

My Commitment

_____

_____

_____

_____

My Next Steps

Do What?	By When?

Notes

_____

_____

_____

_____

_____

_____

_____

_____

_____

_____

_____

_____

_____

_____

_____

_____

_____

_____

_____

_____

_____

_____

_____

_____